Science Facts to Surprise You!

by Grace Hansen

ABDO
SEEING IS BELIEVING
Kids

abdopublishing.com

Published by Abdo Kids, a division of ABDO, PO Box 398166, Minneapolis, Minnesota 55439.

Copyright © 2015 by Abdo Consulting Group, Inc. International copyrights reserved in all countries. No part of this book may be reproduced in any form without written permission from the publisher.

Printed in the United States of America, North Mankato, Minnesota.

102014

012015

 THIS BOOK CONTAINS RECYCLED MATERIALS

Photo Credits: AP Images, Corbis, iStock, NASA, Shutterstock, © NASA/Rex Features p.Cover,17

Production Contributors: Teddy Borth, Jennie Forsberg, Grace Hansen

Design Contributors: Laura Rask, Dorothy Toth

Library of Congress Control Number: 2014943785

Cataloging-in-Publication Data

Hansen, Grace.

 Science facts to surprise you! / Grace Hansen.

   p. cm. -- (Seeing is believing)

ISBN 978-1-62970-734-1

Includes index.

1. Science--Miscellanea--Juvenile literature.   2. Curiosities and wonders--Juvenile literature. I. Title.

500--dc23

                    2014943785

Table of Contents

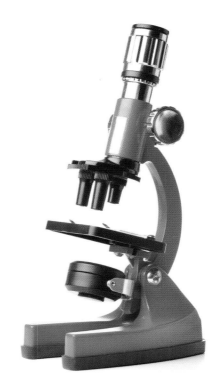

Bad Bugs

Cockroaches are insects.
They are tough. They can
live without their heads!

5

One of a Kind

Everyone's fingerprints are different. All tongue prints are different too!

Your eyes are the same size forever. Your ears and nose grow your entire life.

9

Achoo!

A sneeze can reach speeds of 100 miles per hour (161 km/h)! And about 100,000 germs come out with it.

Spit Machine

Your body makes spit all day, every day. In your life, you will make enough spit to fill a swimming pool!

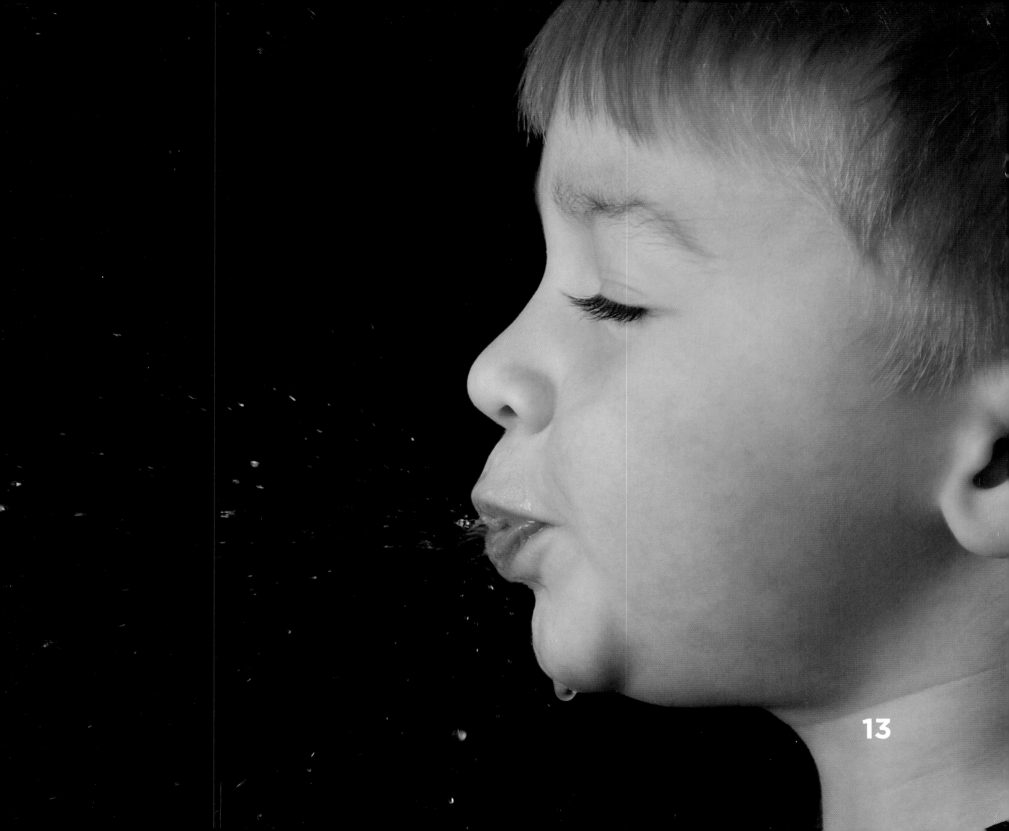

13

Noise-Maker

You can't hum while plugging your nose. Try it!

Space Gas

Astronauts cannot burp in space. On Earth, **gravity** holds food in your stomach. There is no gravity in space. If gas comes up, everything comes up.

Faster Than You Think!

You are always moving, even while standing still. The Earth moves around the sun at 67,000 mph (108,000 km/h). Earth also spins at 1,000 mph (1,600 km/h).

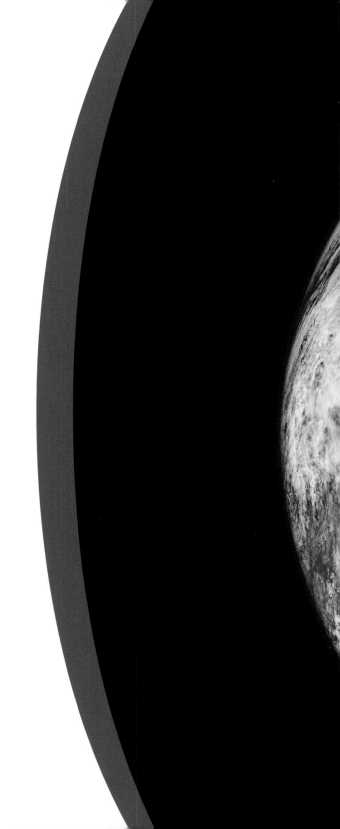

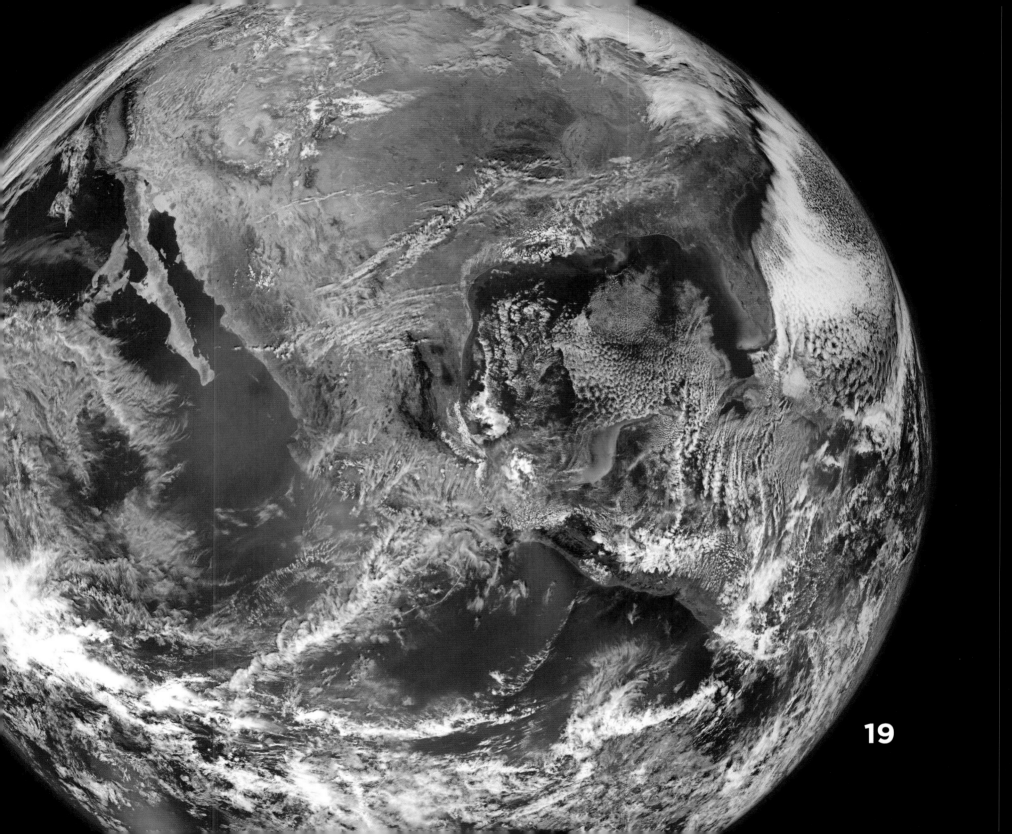

19

Big Heart

The blue whale is the largest animal on Earth. Its heart is the size of a car! You could crawl through the heart's **aorta**.

21

More Facts

- A cockroach can live up to a week without its head. With no head, it breathes through little holes in its body. However, it will die of thirst because it cannot drink.

- Your nose and ears continue to grow because they are made of **cartilage**. Bones stop growing after a certain age, but cartilage keeps on growing.

- The reason you cannot hum while holding your nose is simple. When both your mouth and nose are closed, air cannot pass. When air moves over the vocal cords, they vibrate. When air is not moving, the vibrating stops. The humming sound stops too.

Glossary

aorta – the main and largest artery in the body.
An artery is a tube that sends blood through the body.

cartilage – a flexible and firm tissue. Your ears and
tip of your nose are made of cartilage.

germ – a very small organism that can cause
you to become sick.

gravity – a force that pulls things down.

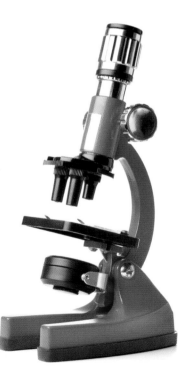

Index

abdokids.com

Use this code to log on to abdokids.com and access crafts, games, videos, and more!

Abdo Kids Code:
SSK7341